EVERYTHING YOU THINK *ABOUT MONEY* IS WRONG

NINE LIES THAT DRIVE
ALL OUR MONEY MISTAKES

CHRIS MCALISTER
with Bret Burchard

1145-J Chesapeake Ave. Columbus, OH 43212

Printed in the United States of America

ISBN: 0989985326
ISBN-13: 978-0989985321

TO DAD.

For teaching me to keep a budget
based on double-entry accounting...
in the tenth grade.

CONTENTS

1
APPEASING THE GODS

As long as humans have organized and religion has developed worldwide, sacrifice has been a key component to dealing with the troubles of life. Whether it has been crops or animals or even people, organized religions have offered sacrifices to the gods and goddesses as a way of ingratiating themselves: a premium calf in exchange for rain so the crops will grow; a choice perfume for food during famine; a mother's firstborn son for protection from the neighboring village on a warpath.

Maybe you don't offer sacrifices to Zeus, but you may be utilizing strategies to ingratiate yourself to someone so things will work out in your favor. The names may have changed, but you are still striving to appease the gods. And you want to appease the gods because you are afraid. Below the surface is a fear that you will be abandoned, that you will not be taken care of, that you will not live up to a given standard, that you will be unworthy and have no place to call home. By addressing this fear through sacrifice, you set up a false illusion of control.

There are no guarantees that things will work out the way we expect them to when it comes to our mission or relationships. As hard as we might try, we cannot keep the storms from entering our lives. But that doesn't stop us from trying anyway!

Where Does This Come From?

Growing up, I caught the idea that God was like a magic genie when it came to money. If I gave enough to God, then everything would work out. And, for a while, it did work that way. I married at 21, and my wife and I set up a budget to give back to God "what was already His", as we were taught. We lived in a radical way, participating in special offerings and giving above and beyond what is traditionally expected. Things worked out well. We built our first home before we had kids and made 30 percent equity the day we moved into the house. The outcomes reinforced the giving scheme.

Then, the truth hit.

In my early thirties, my giving scheme stopped working. We didn't stop giving, but our magic genie stopped producing. We experienced a financial crisis unlike anything ever before. I was substitute teaching just to make ends meet and made in one day about a third of what we needed to pay bills and stock groceries. For me, as a man and a provider, it was crushing.

I questioned everything I believed about giving. Eventually, I did stop giving for a season. I was confused about how God takes care of us. I wasn't making enough money to even keep the car filled with gas. How was I supposed to give? And where was God in all of this? Had I angered the gods somehow?

I want to help you avoid the dangerous thinking that set me up for this crisis. My relationship with God and money was built on ingratiating myself to a higher power. I believed a lie that if I gave to God, then externally I would be covered, but that's not how it works.

My true generosity was blocked by the fear dominating

my heart and the lies I believed about how things were supposed to work out.

Most of us have a desire to be generous. But as we face the reality of what it takes to do so, we see a gap between what we can do and what we want to do. What you may not realize is there is one idea, one way you relate to money, one dominating emotion that blocks that generosity you want to practice. The obstacle is not earning more money or having a better job. The obstacle is a fear suffocating what could be a healthy relationship to money.

You may be in a place financially where you feel like you're suffocating. There never seems to be enough money in the bank account. There is never enough security with your job. You are spread too thin.

Or, perhaps you live comfortably, but you're always afraid of the unexpected.

Or, maybe you (falsely) believe your bank account will always grow.

No matter which of these describes you, it's not a good place to be. How you got there may be a result of habits in your life or choices you have made, or it may be the result of circumstances beyond your control. For most of us, it's a combination of both.

Underneath those decisions or circumstances is a lie you believe about yourself and about God. For insight into how those lies affect how we relate to money, we turn to the story of Zacchaeus, a man entangled in cheating and transformed to be generous.

2
A CONTEXT FOR CHEATERS

In first-century Israel, the atmosphere was one of fear. Rome had become the reigning empire by military conquest built on a massive army and an ingenious "peace plan."

The Roman military would approach a town with a proposition for peace, but this peace wasn't free. The tradeoff was the town had to worship Caesar as Lord and pay him a tax tribute. For Jewish people devoted to God this was not acceptable.

Rome imposed such an oppressive tax scheme that parents could go to debtor's prison and children sold as slaves. At best families could end up selling off their land or losing their businesses because they could not keep up with the tax. Unfortunately, the alternative was no better. Those who refused to succumb to Rome's control were tortured on a cross for inciting revolt. In some areas, crucified people lined the entrance to the village as a reminder of the cost of saying no to peace. So it wasn't long before those in Rome's path ceded to its standards and as a result had to accept taxation.

Oppressive as the tax burden was, there was a way to benefit under it. Rome allowed members of the native population to bid for the position of tax collectors. The tax collectors swindled money away from the people for Rome, and while doing so, took care of themselves as well. It goes without saying these people were feared and hated in their towns. Know how our culture feels about the IRS? Multiply that tenfold, and you will get some idea how these people were regarded.

So here is where we meet Zacchaeus, the tax collector in the region of Jericho, wealthy and hated. He was regarded as all tax collectors were: vile sinners, keeping Israel under oppression.

3
FIND **ME**

In Luke 19, Jesus is making his way through Jericho, and people line the streets to catch a glimpse of Him. Zacchaeus wants to see Jesus, but he's too short to see over the crowds. How is he going to get a glimpse of the rabbi?

When you're the chief tax collector in the town, people don't just part ways to let you walk through. You are the vilest of the vile, and they would prefer you go away. You are a walking representation of why God wasn't seemingly blessing your nation, Israel, and you were helping the enemy. The hate towards you was intertwined with all of the nation's political and religious convictions.

It was in this desperate moment that transformation begins for Zacchaeus. Here's a powerful, wealthy businessman with an abundance of resources—everything except what he really wants, which is to see Jesus. So, seeking a sightline, Zacchaeus runs ahead of Jesus' path and climbs a sycamore fig tree.

Don't miss what this signifies. In Western culture, we focus on rights and freedom, but the focus in Eastern culture is about honor and dignity. In first-century Palestine, a grown man – especially the chief tax collector – does not run. Life waits on him. He is never late, never early, and never in a hurry. And he certainly does not climb trees. But that's exactly what Zacchaeus does. He tosses aside his dignity, runs and climbs in order to catch a glimpse of Jesus.

Then it happened: Jesus sees him and calls him by name.

Consider what occurs in Zacchaeus at this moment. A man already shamed by his role in society, scurrying to see Jesus, not necessarily hoping Jesus sees him. Then the holiest one in the city calls him by name, singles him out from the rest of the crowd. Exposed. He cannot hide any longer.

I imagine Zacchaeus expected to hear words of disappointment or scorn. "Zacchaeus! I am so disappointed with you. You have let me down, stealing from your own people. Can you not see how horrible you are and how horrible you treat these people? You are defective and bad. I can't hang out with you until you cede to my beliefs regarding how bad cheating is." Or "Quit your job. Be ceremonially purified and then I can be with you." If it played out this way the crowd watching would have burst into applause at what they interpreted as righteousness.

But that's not what happens, is it? Instead, Zacchaeus hears, "Zacchaeus, come down immediately. I must stay at your house today."

Once again, we might miss the weight of this exchange if we read through the lens of Western culture. In the Eastern culture, for someone to come to your house was a message that you were loved and accepted. It was a sign of approval. Thus, by calling Zacchaeus out among the crowd, Jesus restores honor and dignity where there was shame.

In response, Zacchaeus quickly climbs down the tree and gladly welcomes Jesus. At this, the people are puzzled and start muttering to themselves. Doesn't the Teacher know who this man is? Doesn't He know Zacchaeus is a sinner?

Imagine this playing out in your community. The most admired person, spending time with the most despised — not to fix the person, but to celebrate him. By going to his house, Jesus is celebrating Zacchaeus.

Fully experiencing the kindness of Jesus in his home, Zacchaeus responds by giving away half of his possessions to the poor. And he doesn't stop there. He also promises to repay anyone he has cheated four times as much as he owes them. To this Jesus responds, "Today salvation has come to this house." Further, Jesus affirms Zacchaeus' true identity as a son of Abraham. A son belonging to the lineage of God's people is the very thing those around Zacchaeus would have said he could not be. This identity was not earned. It was given as a gift and exactly what Zacchaeus longed for.

A Cautionary Note

Be careful not to extrapolate this into your own life too directly or too literally. What happens here is specific to Zacchaeus' needs, but Jesus meets each of us where we are.

I do not parent all three of my children identically; they're different people who need different parenting, based on their unique journey. Your heavenly Father knows the same truth about you, just as Jesus knew it about Zacchaeus. The rich young ruler in the gospel of Mark needed to hear "give it all away," but that's not true for everyone. In fact, in the record we have, Jesus doesn't actually command Zacchaeus to do anything. Zacchaeus instead responds as an overflow of experiencing the delight of Jesus. He isn't trying to earn anything from Jesus, for Jesus is already in his house. Knowing Jesus already accepts him even before he's cleaned up the junk in his life, Zacchaeus practices generosity. This is generosity unblocked.

This is partly why, when it comes to giving, conversations about percentages can do more harm than good. God offers Himself to us. We offer all back. We discern where to give, where to spend, where to save, and where to invest. It is a personalized and relational approach that transcends doves, garden herbs (Matthew 23), and any sort of God tax.

Luke 19:10 says, "For the Son of Man came to seek and to save the lost." Jesus wants to find you. We need to allow ourselves to be found. It is not about how much you go to church. It is not about how much you read your Bible. It is not about how you can make your life appear holy. It is not about how much you give. While these actions can be helpful, the primary focus is on letting yourself intimately, completely be found.

Too often we approach Jesus like Zacchaeus did, hoping to catch a glimpse of Him but hoping He does not see us, fearful of the scorning words from a disappointed Father. If God is not a gentle, loving Father... a close brother in the Son, Jesus...and an intimate, loving Spirit, then He has been remade in the image of your shame.

The way of Jesus is to seek and to find. The way of humanity is to allow ourselves to be found. From acceptance, celebration, and delight, then, flows transformed generosity.

4
A ZACCHAEUS **MOMENT**

Jesus said much about leveraging your money, time, energy, relationships, and resources for the Kingdom. The superficial response to this invitation is a reduction to managing money well. There is good in managing well but how you relate to money can still be fundamentally flawed. Simply managing money better does not unblock the flow of generosity. Contrary to popular teaching, our hearts do not follow our money. If that were true, the Pharisees' habit of tithing would have transformed them. You can't correct the root by propping up new fruit. Internal transformation is first and this will overflow external changes.

For the follower of Christ, the Holy Spirit is developing fruit in and through us. So what's blocking your fruit-bearing when it comes to money and generosity?

There are nine lies and nine truths[1] regarding how we see ourselves and how God sees us. These lies impact every area of our lives, including how we interact with money. You may see some of yourself in each of these, but as you examine them closer, one will stand out as the dominant core fear for you. When you recognize the lie you believe about who you are, you can learn to receive the truth about who God says you are. Then, transformation happens.

The Lie of the Debit Card

You may approach life like you approach your debit card. You use it but ignore the strings attached to it. If this is you, you are like Zacchaeus before meeting Jesus. You don't believe that God radically loves you for who you are; you believe He can only love you if you manage your money wisely. This lie fosters insecurity in your heart that causes you to use money to manipulate others in order to feel love. You may appear generous, offering many gifts, but there always seem to be strings attached to the gifts.

If this sounds familiar, you need the fruit of the spirit of love. When you experience the Father's delight in you as Zacchaeus experienced, you won't need to manipulate others to get love, nor will you allow yourself to be continually manipulated.

The Lie of the Credit Card

Have you ever found comfort by spending money or escaped by maxing out the credit card? The pain was throbbing. You felt suffocated by the lie that you have to be self-reliant. Somewhere you experienced abandonment, and now you believe you have to take care of yourself. The pain of isolation and loneliness is your only friend, and you escape through spending money. You believe a lie that you will only experience joy through another human being as your perfect caretaker.

The truth is that joy comes when you hear the Father say, "I'm coming to your house today! I want to hang out with you!" You may still experience moments when you externally feel like you will not be taken care of, but when you receive the fruit of the spirit of joy, you realize that internally, you have everything you need in Jesus. You were designed for perfect caretaking available only in one place.

The Lie of the Shopping Spree

This lie is closely related to credit and debit cards. You

spend money in order to feel better. It works like a drug. You self-indulge with your money, and it works like a high. When you feel you do not have a unique place in the world, you are positioned to struggle with this; when self-indulgence becomes the pattern of your relationship with money, it will destroy your life.

It is painful to wonder if anyone really ever sees you. It hurts to feel like everyone is looking past you or ignoring you – as they did with Zacchaeus. But Jesus saw him, and Jesus sees you. You're not invisible to Him.

When you receive affirmation from the Father that you are seen for who you uniquely are, that you are loved and that you are adopted into God's family, then you no longer need to self-indulge. You receive the fruit of the spirit of self-control.

The Lie of Ignoring Bills

You're caught in this lie if your response to money problems is to just ignore them. If you keep kicking the can farther down the road and delay paying that bill, you falsely believe it might just go away. This is your attempt to create peace, but it is an artificial peace. You feel like you don't really belong anywhere, or your presence does not matter. You are overwhelmed with a sense of disconnection; you believe your problems would go away if you had a place to belong. So you look the other way, while you deteriorate financially.

You need the fruit of the spirit of peace – real peace. But this peace doesn't mean your problems all go away; you'll always have problems. This peace comes in when Jesus enters your home. When you receive His peace, it changes the way you relate to money. It brings about the courage to face reality fiercely and make changes.

The Lie of Money "Mastery"

Your lie may not be any of the above. You may be a master of money. You have a sound budget and rarely stray from it. You are succeeding with money management. You are a champion of your finances. It's another part of your life that's unmanageable.

Perhaps your home life is in shambles. Maybe you don't get along with one of your kids or your marriage is coasting downhill. At some point, you've believed a lie that you are incompetent and do not have what it takes. Your response is to specialize in one area of your life. Why step into areas where you might lose when you're thriving in areas where you win?

Folks like Zacchaeus who have their spreadsheet perfected usually have another area of their life that is neglected. They only want to invest in categories of life they are assured they can perform well. They don't want to experience the displeasure of others or let themselves down making the necessary mistakes needed to grow.

You need to experience the patience of God. He is patient with you. He is willing to spend all the time needed at your house hanging out like he did with Zacchaeus. He is patient while you learn to apply your passion and skills in money management to other areas of your life. You have all the time you need. When you receive the fruit of the spirit of patience you give yourself permission to step out into new ventures and grow.

The Lie of Net Worth

You are not your net worth. You believe the more money you have, the more worthy you are. If you have little then you are worth little. If that is the hamster wheel you're spinning on then you will never have enough. When your worth is connected to your performance, you falsely perceive God as a taskmaster. You falsely think He evaluates you only by performance. When you believe God only delights in you when you perform well with money or behave a certain way, then you need the fruit of the spirit of kindness. God's kindness means His delight in you isn't connected to how much money you do or don't have.

Jesus delighted in Zacchaeus while he was still a corrupt tax collector, before his heart or his money habits changed. Jesus loved Zacchaeus regardless of how much or how little he had. When you realize you are worthy for who you are, not for what you achieve, then you begin to deconstruct the lie that more money equals more worth. This doesn't mean you'll no longer want to make more money—nor should it, necessarily. There is nothing wrong with wanting to make money. Just keep in mind that making or losing money doesn't define who you are. The kindness of God means you are loved regardless of your net worth. Your Heavenly Father defines kindness. His kindness, expressed through Jesus and experienced in the Spirit, defines you. Your accumulation of wealth does not.

The Lie of a "Transaction Report"

If you are constantly critical of the way you spend money, you believe a lie that you are defective, and that God is mad at you because you do not manage your money better. But Jesus looks on you like He did Zacchaeus. He wants to hang out with you! He wants to come to your house today!

If you're constantly tearing yourself down, you need the fruit of the spirit of goodness. God loves you. In Jesus you are not bad, defective, or corrupt. He gives you His divine nature. When you believe internally that you are good, you will stop constantly criticizing your use of money. The energy you spend being critical will be transformed to help you be creative, to pursue new income streams, to take what you have and multiply it. You can spend your energy beating yourself up over a lie, or you can spend it cooperating with the truth of how God wants to grow you.

The Lie of "Giving = Getting Back"

Perhaps you are like I was in my twenties, believing that if I tithed I would never struggle. It worked for a while, but it was not an attachment to God. It was an attachment to a false belief.

Jesus loved Zacchaeus whether he gave money or not, and Jesus loves you whether you give money or not.

We falsely believe tithing is a blanket protection from financial chaos. But if your mind dwells on the worst-case scenarios of what might happen to you, there will never be enough commas or zeroes in your bank account to help you feel real peace. You are crippled by the anxiety that you may reach a point when you do not have enough, so you stay overly alert to your money.

If you've bought this lie, you need to receive the fruit of the spirit of faithfulness. God is faithful. Internally, you can rest in Him as your Father, regardless of what happens externally. There can be internal peace when there is external chaos.

The Lie of "My Financial Plan Is My Business"

No one can tell you what you should do with your money. Rigidly you falsely believe you don't need their help. You bristle at the thought of receiving any advice regarding your money because that feels like they have some control over you. You have made some bad choices and want to over-assert your independence by rebelling against healthy financial systems. The bottom line is that you've been betrayed and dare not let anyone too close even if you need financial wisdom because they will hurt you. Perhaps you even drum up arguments about money with those you love to confirm those self-sabotaging suspicions.

If this sounds like where you are mentally you need to receive the fruit of the spirit of gentleness. God is gentle. The purpose of His power isn't to overpower you but empower you. Zacchaeus wasn't scared by Jesus into paying back others where he had cheated them. His experience with Jesus being safe allowed him to overflow the generosity he had received.

Jesus has brought you into the family. He wants to come to your house. Your good, perfect, and gentle Heavenly Father will never betray you. This relaxes you to receive wisdom from others who are skilled and discerning regarding the use of money.

5
YOUR FINANCIAL *HOME*

Most of us are trying to get money to do for us what Jesus has already done through the cross and made available by the Spirit. But there's good news: you don't have to be a victim of the lies you believe and fear you feel regarding money.

Money cannot give you what you really need. Money cannot say to you, "Zacchaeus, I'm coming to your house today." It cannot say, "I delight in you." It cannot offer you joy. It cannot offer you peace. It cannot offer you faithfulness. It cannot meet your core needs.

Who you are is defined by Jesus. Only He can call your name out loud amongst the crowds in a life-giving way. No one else, nothing else, can give you the name you need.

When you allow yourself to be found, you can be generous, knowing God is already happy with you. God already loves you abundantly. He delights in you. When you rest in that truth, you will overflow in generosity because you have everything you need in Him, in abundance.

The question is not how can you become more generous. The question is what is blocking your generosity? What lie do you believe that keeps you from living a generous lifestyle? Once you identify the lie, you can resist it and grow beyond it as you are found...just as Zacchaeus was.

Getting Started

There are a few ways you can maximize the unblocking of generosity.

First, receive the courage to step into the fear that blocks your generosity. What are you afraid of? You will find on the other side that you can't out imagine how good God really is in finding you. Don't get distracted by the shallow conversation of money micro-management. This can be built on fear when stewardship becomes scrooge-ship.

Second, get financial coaching. There are people who have done and are doing what you want to do. Seek their advice.

Finally, set up a budgeting system for yourself. My children use a bank with three sections: save, share, and spend. When we give them their allowance, we teach them to divide their money accordingly, and in the process we hope they learn to be wise with their money. Note that we're not setting them up for an existential crisis. They know that Mom and Dad love them no matter what happens with their finances. (Oh and I'll be bribing them to learn how to use their savings wisely. Investing their savings in skill development beats passive savings.)

Maybe you're like me and need something more sophisticated than a piggy bank. Some use an envelope method or spreadsheet. Find what works for you.

Bottom line: budgeting is not about making payments to buy God's favor. Budgeting is just a tool to help all of us be wise.

God wants to come to your financial house today. And mine, too.

I used to wonder how hard life must be for the people on the side of the road pushing carts containing all of their belongings. When I was facing eviction and could not even buy a box of Cheerios, I feared I would soon be one of those people. I was aware of that fear and leaned into it, receiving the truth Jesus was offering. He helped me deconstruct the lie I believed about money and what it could give me. He affirmed the truth that I was worthy and loved, regardless of my performance as a provider. It unblocked my generosity, and our family started giving again, even when it didn't seem to make sense.

Remember, the first home my wife and I lived in we had built – at age 21! We walked in on day one with over 30% equity. I started contributing to a retirement account at age 20. All that being said, if my finances had worked out the way I wanted them to at that young age, I would see everything regarding money through a lens of "you should have known better," "you should have tried harder," and "you should have given more money to a church...err...to God."

Instead, I walked into a foolish business decision that, in five years, put me on the hook for over seven zeroes. I became financially insolvent and spent eight hellish years climbing out of a hole. Now, I realize everything I thought about money was wrong. I thought if I wrote a check to God, my finances would always be taken care of. I had to learn the hard way, like Zacchaeus. I could not "give" my way into a changed heart. I needed to know God loved me wildly--that regardless of what I did with money, God wanted to hang out with me.

Now, I can pay my kids their allowances and teach them financial principles. But I make sure they know that God and I love them regardless of how they use their money. I can tell them about the hole we have climbed out of and even say no to things when it is a tight week financially. But, because I do not have to feel fear in regard to my finances, I can protect them from the intensity of fearful overreactions on my part that would make them feel shame. "You bought what?!?!"

Regardless of our circumstances, our relationships to money can change when our relationships to God and ourselves change. We become transformed internally by the abundance of God...and overflowing generosity happens.

Jesus delights in you. When you, like Zacchaeus, allow yourself to be truly, authentically, and passionately found -- when you face the lies you believe with courage -- you will unblock the generosity welling up inside you, a generosity that comes from your perfect Father.

Afterword

Our relationship to money changes when we change. We change when fear loses its power. Sharing with one safe person the fear you feel regarding money can aid your liberation. Voice the lie you have falsely come to believe about God. Confession helps loosen the grip of fear. Share what you have read and realized about yourself with someone. Check out the book SightShift: Identity for more help.

Note 1*

I am attempting to rework contributions from fields of personality development and typology. Early on I was influenced by the Riso book. After I had already done work making a larger Biblical connection I discovered the book by Richard Rohr that may be helpful to you:

Riso, Don Richard and Russ Hudson. 1999. The wisdom of the enneagram. New York City: Bantam.

Rohr, Richard and Andreas Ebert. 2011. The enneagram: a Christian perspective. New York: CrossRoad Publishing.

sight shift

SightShift events empower individuals with a paradigm for living confident, clear minded, and an enjoyment of healthy relationships. Events are designed to facilitate a shift in how you see God and your self. Options for event speaking, day long training or multiple-day retreats are available. Learn more...

SIGHTSHIFT.COM/ EVENTS

MarriageShift

SightShift for couples. MarriageShift includes resources, seminars and training for married couples. Experience security in Jesus, gain clarity in your role as a spouse and foster a life-giving, intimate relationship. Find out more...

MARRIAGESHIFT.COM

SightShift: Lead

SightShift: lead events are designed for individuals and teams to lead with full engagement. We've watched these transform organizations, leadership teams and volunteers. Options for event speaking, day long training or multiple-day retreats are available. Learn more...

SIGHTSHIFT.COM/ LEAD

SightShift: Champion

SightShift: Champion exists to spread the SightShift message in the arena of competitive athletics, focused on helping coaches and athletes learn to achieve the highest levels of performance while fostering strength in who they are.

SIGHTSHIFT.COM/CHAMPION

Made in the USA
Monee, IL
05 November 2026

67382336R00021